Bitcoin

Mastering the Digital Cryptocurrency Gold

Alex M Peter

©2018

information is without contract or any type of guarantee assurance.

The trademarks that are used are without any consent, and the publication of the trademark is without permission or backing by the trademark owner. All trademarks and brands within this book are for clarifying purposes only and are the owned by the owners themselves, not affiliated with this document.

Table of Contents

Introduction

Welcome to the world of Bitcoin. You have found the right book that discusses everything that you need to know to get started with Bitcoin. Whether you are interested in finally getting into the digital currency market or you would like to learn how you can use this currency to help you get ahead with your investment or business, this guidebook will provide you with the tools and information that you need to get started.

In this guidebook, you will find the various aspects of Bitcoin that you need to know to use it properly. We will start with some basics such as what is Bitcoin, how the blockchain technology behind Bitcoin works, how to exchange your traditional currency out for Bitcoin, and even where you can make purchases with your new Bitcoin. We will also take a look at the future of Bitcoin and how to keep your coins safe from hackers.

There is so much to learn when you decide to start using Bitcoin. The network is always growing, and more people are joining it each day. When you are ready to learn more about Bitcoin, and you are considering whether to join the network or not, make sure to read through this guidebook before you jump in.

Chapter 1: What Is Bitcoin?

Digital currencies are starting to take over the world. The idea behind these digital currencies is pretty new, and just a few years ago, people would have laughed at the idea of being able to work with a currency that is only available online, can be used across borders, and doesn't have a central authority controlling it. Today, there are more than a thousand digital currencies that are available, but one of the most recognized and most widely used one is Bitcoin.

Bitcoin was one of the first digital currencies that broke out to the market. It was created in 2009, by an anonymous group or person who goes by the name of Satoshi Nakamoto. This currency came out at the perfect time. Just the year before, many countries throughout the world had gone through an economic downturn, and they felt like they could not trust their government or big financial institutions to take care of their money. Some of the ideas that came with Bitcoin appealed to these people, and it quickly took off from there.

Bitcoin is a digital currency that is created and held electronically. There isn't anyone who controls it so you will not have to worry about a bank or a government taking over and changing the rules. Instead, Bitcoin relies on a mathematical equation and the blockchain to keep it going and secure. The coins that you use on this network can't be printed, so you will not be able to go to an ATM or another source to get them like you can with Euros or dollars. Instead, people or businesses who are known as miners will solve mathematical equations to release more Bitcoin into the market.

One question that many beginners have is how Bitcoin is different from normal currencies and how it can be the same. To start, Bitcoin is usually used to purchase things electronically. Users on the network can search for companies that accept Bitcoin and then exchange their coins for items. In this way, Bitcoin is very similar to using your dollars or Euros online to make purchases as well. If this is the main reason that you want to use Bitcoin, you are not going to see much difference in using it compared to using your traditional currency, other than there are fewer stores that accept it.

However, the biggest difference with Bitcoin and one of the reasons that many people are flocking to this digital currency is that it is decentralized. You do not have to deal with one single institution controlling the network. People like this idea because there isn't a big bank or another entity that is controlling their money and they are more likely to complete their transactions without everyone online knowing who they are.

Who created Bitcoin?

It is uncertain about who is the original creator of Bitcoin. Satoshi Nakamoto is considered a software developer who proposed Bitcoin and the idea of creating an electronic payment system that would be based on a mathematical proof rather than any entity controlling it. The idea here is that the currency would occur all online, the transactions could happen electronically, there wouldn't be issues with a central authority, and if there were any transaction fees, they would be very low.

While the developer (or group of people) went under the name of Satoshi Nakamoto and released several white papers on how Bitcoin should be used, no one knows who really started this currency. This is most likely done on purpose to keep people out of the running of Bitcoin as much as possible.

Can I print the coins?

No, it is not possible to print out any of the coins. This currency is not like traditional currencies that you can print out, and you will not be able to go to a central bank to get more of the currency. Instead, the Bitcoin network was created by a community of people, and it is a network that anyone who wants to can join. While you can print out the private key to your Bitcoin to keep it safe from hackers, you will not be able to print off any bills and take them along with you.

The Bitcoin network is also designed to only have so many coins available right from the start. When Bitcoin was designed, there was only 21 million Bitcoin available in total, but not all of them were released at once. As the miners went and did their work, more coins would be released, allowing for the currency to grow without a central authority in place.

While other currencies are going to be based on silver or gold, Bitcoin is not based on any of these. Bitcoin is actually reliant on software and mathematical equations to keep it going. Anyone who would like to check it out can see the mathematical formula that is being used, and since it is open sourced, anyone can look to make sure that it is behaving properly. This adds in some transparency to the whole network as well.

What are some of the characteristics of Bitcoin?

You will notice that Bitcoin offers a few unique characteristics that make it a great choice for many around the world to use. Some of these characteristics include:

- It's decentralized: This means that there isn't a central authority around that will control how this currency works. Each machine that mines the Bitcoin or joins the network will help make decisions.

- Easy to set up: While it may be hard to set up a bank account at your local financial institution, you can get your own Bitcoin account, and Bitcoin coins, set up in just a matter of minutes.

- Anonymous: You will receive a Bitcoin address (you can also decide what the address should be), which will help to protect your information online.

- Transparent: All of the transactions that ever occur on this network are stored on the blockchain, and anyone on the network can take a look at the blockchain whenever they would like.

- Low transaction fees: While big banks often charge large fees to complete transactions, the transaction fees are minimal to nothing on the Bitcoin network.

- Fast: It is possible to send and receive money in a matter of minutes when you use the Bitcoin network. Compared to waiting a few days to do this through your bank or other financial institution, this can be a nice change.

As you can see, when you use Bitcoin as a payment method, it may seem very similar to using the American dollar or another traditional currency, except that you are only able to use Bitcoin online. There are also a number of other benefits to working with Bitcoin that you just can't find with your traditional currencies. This helps to make Bitcoin a popular choice and is one of the many reasons that the value of Bitcoin has gone through the roof.

Chapter 2: The Blockchain Technology Behind Bitcoin

While many people enjoy all the freedom that they can get from using Bitcoin, and they like that there isn't a big government agency that is taking care of their money, there are still some issues with this kind of network. You still need to have some method of adding security, transparency, and trust in the network. Since Bitcoin network occurs online, how do you ensure that the transactions are being completed, that no one is messing with the information and that everything is in its place?

The developers of Bitcoin realized that they needed to add something to make sure that the network has transparency and still offers security. If there was the risk that someone would be able to mess around with the transactions on the network or steal the information from the users, it would be much harder to convince anyone to use it. They would just stick with their traditional banking system rather than making any changes.

This is why the blockchain technology has been developed. The blockchain is basically a ledger. It can hold onto any information of value, but it is used to hold onto the transactions that occur on the Bitcoin network, as well as with the other digital currencies that you may choose to work with.

All users who join the Bitcoin network will be a part of this blockchain technology. They will receive a part of a chain that will hold onto all the transactions that they complete on the network. As they do more transactions, they will fill up the chain and then miners will come in and provide a unique code to the chain. This keeps the information all in line but ensures that no one can go and steal your personal information. Transactions on this network are almost instant, they are secure, and they are really easy to work with.

Because of this blockchain technology, the Bitcoin network was able to take off and do really well. People found that it was easy to use and that it would be easy to keep their personal information safe. It was an even better option compared to some of the traditional methods that are used by online banks and even online stores.

There are actually many different ways that the blockchain technology can be used. It was originally released to work with Bitcoin and other digital currencies, but it has since been developed to be used in a variety of other places as well. Many banks and financial institutions, insurance agencies, and more have developed their own blockchain application because they like how easy it is to use and how much it can help them provide better customer service no matter what industry they are in.

Chapter 3: The Pros and Cons of Bitcoins

The value of Bitcoin has quickly risen in value. Within one year, the value of Bitcoin went from about $2000 a coin to over $14,000, and at one point it almost reached a value of $19000. This is a huge increase and has quickly helped Bitcoin, as well as other digital currencies, gain in popularity in no time. For those who have never used a cryptocurrency before, it may be confusing why you would want to use these coins. You may be asking what the benefits and negatives of these coins are all about. Let's take a look at these benefits and negatives so you can decide if digital currencies are the right option for you.

The benefits of using Bitcoins

There are a lot of reasons why you may want to choose to work with Bitcoin and other digital currencies, rather than relying on your traditional currency. The market for these currencies is growing, which is why the value has seen tremendous growth over the past few years. Some of the benefits of using Bitcoin include:

- **Available anywhere in the world**: Anyone, anywhere in the world can use Bitcoin. As long as they have access to the internet and can switch out their local currency, they can be a part of this network. This makes for a very large demographic for using Bitcoin and helps to increase its value.

- **Privacy:** While some of the exchange sites will ask for some personal information because it is required in the country you live in for tax reasons, you can remain anonymous when using the Bitcoin network. This can be a nice change to some of the other payment methods you may have used in the past. You can make purchases, send money, and even receive money without others knowing any of your personal information.

- **Fast transactions:** When you work with your traditional bank, you have probably noticed that it can take a few days for transactions to process through. This can be frustrating in a world where a lot of other things can be instant. With Bitcoin, you can use the blockchain technology to send and receive money in a matter of seconds, rather than waiting several days.

- **Low fees:** Unlike when working with a bank or other financial institution, you will not have to pay large fees to send money or complete transactions with Bitcoin. The blockchain technology can do all the work in a few minutes for you for no cost.

- **No central authority running it**: Another reason that you may want to work with Bitcoin rather than your traditional currency is that there is no bank, government, or other central authority running the currency. With the economic issues that plagued the world in 2008, many people started losing their trust in how well their government could manage the currency. This is about the time that Bitcoin was started and seems to be a big reason that people are joining the network. Bitcoin is run on a mathematical equation and the blockchain technology, so it is safe and easy to use without having to rely on any government entity messing around.

- **Easy to use:** Many people like to go with Bitcoin because it is really easy to use. You simply need to find a good exchange site, change out your traditional currency for the Bitcoins and then start using them. Whether you would like to invest your coins, use them right away for purchases, or something else, this network is one of the easiest payment methods around.

Working with Bitcoin is becoming widely accepted. There are even some major companies who will now accept Bitcoin as a form of payment just like they accept cash or credit cards. As more people throughout the world start to rely on Bitcoin and accept it, it is likely to continue growing and growing, adding more benefits than ever before.

The negatives of Bitcoins

There are a lot of reasons why you would want to choose Bitcoin over one of the other digital currencies out there or over your traditional currencies. However, using digital currencies is not something that will work well for everyone. Some people may not like the risk that comes with this currency, or they don't like how volatile these currencies can be. Some of the negatives to using Bitcoin compared to a traditional currency include:

- **Very volatile**: While the overall trend of Bitcoin is currently going upwards, there has been a lot of up and down movement with the currency. If you look at some of the charts for Bitcoin, it rarely stays in the same spot and can go from big highs to low lows in no time at all. This can make it hard to figure out the value of your currency.

- **Has a high risk:** There are a lot of risks when it comes to using Bitcoin. Unlike traditional currencies, the value of digital currencies can quickly go up and down without much notice. If you are an investor or even just a regular user of Bitcoin, you may find that your coins will go down quickly and you have less than you started out with.

- **Can lose value quickly:** Another risk you may face with Bitcoin is that it can lose value very quickly. There isn't any government holding it up so it often depends on the level of trust from the users for how much value it will have. There have recently been several countries who have banned the use of Bitcoin, which has dropped the value significantly. For businesses, users, and even investors, this can be bad news because you want the currency to keep going up.

- **No protection:** While it is a benefit that there isn't a central authority that is in control of the currency, this can spell disaster in some cases. Without someone controlling the currency, you have no protection if something goes wrong. If a hacker gets onto your wallet or there is a computer glitch, you could lose all your coins, and no one is there to help you. If the value of the currency goes down quickly, no one is there to save it. You have to decide whether the risk is worth it or not before joining this network.

While there are a lot of benefits to using Bitcoin instead of a traditional currency, you also have to remember that it is not a choice that will work for everyone. Learn about the positives and negatives of using Bitcoin so you can make the right decision for your needs.

Chapter 4: How to Buy and Store Bitcoin?

To get started on the Bitcoin network, you need to make sure that you purchase some coins and set up your own Bitcoin address. Once you do these two things (which are pretty simple to accomplish), you will be able to send and receive money and make all the purchases that you would like. Let's take a look at how you can get started with purchasing your own coins on this network.

First, we need to get a Bitcoin address. You can choose to go on to the Bitcoin network and do this, but most people decide to get their address through an exchange site. This makes things a little bit easier because you can also do an exchange of your coins at the same time. There are a few different exchange sites that are available for you to choose from, but the most popular one in the United States for Bitcoin is Coinbase.

So, let's look at signing up for Coinbase. This is a pretty easy process to go through. You just need to go to coinbase.com and then put in the information that they request. This is pretty basic information for you to put in, such as your name and some verification information. This one has not gotten to the point of needing as much information as some of the other websites, so it is pretty simple to go through and set up an account.

Once you have done all of the steps, including verifying your email account so that you can get messages from Coinbase, you will be able to visit the main page from there. This main page will have a lot of information that can be useful as you get started with Bitcoin. First, you will be able to notice that there is some information on the current exchange rates of Bitcoin, Litecoin, and Ethereum. If you would like to work with these currencies, you can do this through Coinbase as well.

You also need to take time to add in a payment method. This allows you to send in some traditional currency to exchange for Bitcoin. There are a few options that you can use, and the verification process does take a few days to complete, but it will get easier once you set up the method.

Picking the method, you would like to use will be based on personal preference. Right now, Coinbase will accept bank account, credit or debit card, or PayPal. The first method to use is your bank account. This method is a good one because it is pretty simple to use and will allow you to exchange larger amounts of money. If you want to make a big purchase or invest a lot of money in the market, then the bank account is the method to go with. One negative though is that it will take about three to five days for a transaction to go through. This is mostly because of the way that your bank handles the transactions. If you want to do your transactions quickly, you need to pick one of the other methods.

PayPal and a credit card are other options that you can use. These methods usually finish up the transaction within a day, but your limits for exchanging will be lower than what you can do with your bank account. These methods may also require some more personal information to get the transaction complete. But if you are looking to get into the market quickly, they are great options that will speed up transaction time.

Working with the Bitcoin network is a really simple process. Going through the steps above are really only going to take a few minutes to complete, and as soon as you have picked out and verified your payment method, you will be able to exchange your currencies either direction whenever you would like!

Storing your Bitcoin

Once you have purchased your Bitcoin, it is time to find a place to store them. You will not be able to print out the currency like you can with your traditional currency, so you need to have some place to hold onto the coins so that they are available whenever you would like to use them. There are a few options that you can pick from when you are ready to store your Bitcoin, and the method you use will often depend on how often you plan to use the coins. Some of the options that you can use when it comes to storing your Bitcoin include:

- **Online wallet:** The online wallet is the first option that you can choose. It is the most convenient and when you open a Coinbase account, this is where the coins will be sent. If you plan on using the coins right away to make a purchase, the online wallet can be a great option because you will not have to undergo any other steps before using the currency. However, these wallets are more susceptible to hacking so if you want to invest the currency or plan in holding onto the coins for some time, it is best to choose another option.

- **Hardware wallet:** With a hardware wallet, you will move your coins offline and store them in a secure file on your computer. This makes them easy to access when needed but adds a level of security because the private key that holds your coins is no longer online. You can even take it a step further and save this file on a USB drive as well. It takes a bit longer to use these coins since you will need to transfer them back online when needed, but for investors, it can add to the security that you need.

- **Cold storage:** For those who plan to invest in Bitcoin and use the buy and hold strategy, cold storage may be the best option. With this option, you are going to remove the private key completely from your computer by printing it off and storing in another location. This makes it almost impossible for a hacker to get ahold of the information. It takes a bit longer when you want to use the coins, but if you are using the buy and hold strategy, you aren't planning on using the coins all that much anyway.

It is a good idea to pick the right storage for your coins. Some people will even have a few different backup methods, especially when they are investing in the Bitcoin network. Each time that you add more coins to your wallet though, or make major changes, make sure to resave the private key so that it is up to date with the right information.

Chapter 5: How to Make Money with Bitcoin?

While many people join the Bitcoin network to make purchases and complete transactions all over the world, there are some who see the big increases in the value of Bitcoin and see it as a great investment opportunity. There are many ways that you can make money through Bitcoin, and this investment can work whether you have a lot of money or you are a new or more advanced investor. Some of the options that you can use to make money with Bitcoin include:

Mining

The first method that you can use to make money with Bitcoin is mining. Mining is a complex process and can take some time to learn, but if you like programming and working on complex math problems, it could be a good way to make money with Bitcoin. This option is not only going to help you to earn money through the Bitcoin network, but it also helps to keep the transactions safe for other users.

When you are a miner, you will be given a part of the blockchain that is full of transactions. You will then need to go through and make up a code that will protect and hide the transactions on the network. There are a few rules to doing this. You need to make sure that the characters match up with the other parts of the blockchain, that when one character changes it will change all of the other characters that occur behind it, and there must be a certain amount of zeroes at the beginning of each one.

If you are successful, you can earn 25 Bitcoin for the work. This helps to make it appealing for others to work on this and slowly releases more Bitcoin into the market, but it brings in a lot of competition in the process. Many people who work in mining choose to join a group. These groups make things easier because each person will work on just part of the code, rather than all of it, speeding things up and making their income a bit more reliable than doing it all on your own.

Investing

It is common for many people to choose to put their money into Bitcoin to make some profit. Investing is very profitable with Bitcoin, especially since the price is currently going up and is predicted to go even higher in the future. There are a few different options that you can use when it comes to investing in Bitcoin including the following:

The buy and hold strategy

The buy and hold strategy is probably one of the most common investment strategies that you will find with digital currency investing. This is because it is one of the easiest. You basically purchase the amount of Bitcoin that you want to use, place it in a secure wallet, and then just wait. When the value of Bitcoin goes up, you will take the coins and exchange them back for your traditional currency and keep the profit. There isn't a lot of work with this, you will not have to focus on the daily ups and downs of the market, and as long as you watch out for a big downtrend that doesn't reverse, you will make money.

Let's look at an example of how this works. Let's say that back in February of 2017, you purchased one Bitcoin for $2500. At the beginning of January 2018, you could exchange the coins out to your traditional currency, and you would have more than $14,500. This is a $12,000 profit for just leaving the coins in the market for less than a year, and you could choose to stay in the market if you would like.

The most important thing to remember here is that you must store the coins somewhere secure. Using an online wallet is not the best because then you always need to worry about hackers getting ahold of your money. Pick a hardware wallet or a cold storage option and learn how to watch the market and you can make a great profit for very little work with this method.

Investing in the blockchain

There are a lot of applications for using the blockchain technology. While it was first introduced to help Bitcoin be more secure and as the ledger for all transactions that occur on that network. But there are many other ways that you will be able to use this technology, and many investors are choosing to invest in this to help them make money.

There are a variety of companies as well as developers who are working to develop the blockchain technology to work for their needs. Insurance, banks, and anyone who is trying to keep track of various transactions and other things of value can use the blockchain. You can invest some of your money in a developer or a company who is working on a new blockchain application, and then when the application sells and does well, you will earn the money back.

Day trading

Some people will decide to work with day trading to make money with Bitcoin. This method is going to require you to work on a lot of little trades throughout the day, taking advantage of the ups and downs that occur naturally in the market. You will have to constantly watch the market to see when you should enter the trade and when you should leave to make a profit (or limit your losses).

Day trading can be a great way to make a full-time income on Bitcoin, and it can make things easier to leave the market if things start to turn south. You will make a lot of little trades throughout the day, but over time these are going to add up to big profits for you to enjoy if you do it right.

Even though the trend for Bitcoin is going up, if you look at the daily charts, you will notice that the value goes up and down many times through the day. With some research, you will go and look at the average value of the coins. When you see that the coins are available before that market value, you will make a purchase. Then when the coins go above this average, you will sell them and take the profit. The amount that you make on each trade may not be huge, but when you do a lot of them, it can definitely add up.

With day trading, you need to make all of your purchases and sales within the same day. Bitcoin is available in all parts of the world, and it is hard to monitor how the market will do in other parts of the world when you are sleeping. Make sure that if you purchase into a trade on one day that you sell out of it by the end of the day to help protect your investment.

Many people decide to join the Bitcoin network to make money. They see that the value of Bitcoin is quickly going up and they want to be a part of it. Using the methods above will help you to earn money while others are using the Bitcoin network.

Chapter 6: How to Use Bitcoin for Purchases?

Making purchases on the Bitcoin network is actually pretty easy. Once you have set up your own Bitcoin wallet and you have an address, it is simply a matter of visiting the website that you want to use and sending the money over. In many cases, if you followed the steps that we outlined when exchanging your fiat currency over to Bitcoin on Coinbase, you will already have a wallet and everything else that you need.

Let's say that you are ready to purchase with the help of Bitcoin. There are a few methods that you can use. In some of the bigger cities, there are some companies where you can visit in person and make a purchase. These are limited, but they are starting to grow as the acceptability and value of Bitcoin continue to grow.

If you have one of those companies around and they accept Bitcoin, you can easily make a payment right at the cash register. You simply need to download a Bitcoin app to your phone. You will then be able to scan the code from the store into the phone and send over the number of coins. This may sound complicated, but it just requires a scan and a few seconds to make the payment, as long as you have the money in your wallet.

Since most physical stores do not accept Bitcoin yet (even though Bitcoin is growing, it will probably be a few more years before it becomes that widely accepted), most of your Bitcoin purchases will occur online. The good news is that making purchases online with Bitcoin can be pretty simple.

First, you need to find a store that accepts Bitcoin as a form of payment. There are a number of options you can go with, and we listed a few below. Go through and find the products you want to purchase just like normal and fill out the personal information, such as your address and shipping information, like normal. Once you get to a payment method, you can click on the link that the company should provide you to pay for Bitcoin.

After clicking on this link, you should be provided with the Bitcoin address for the company you are using. You can then send over your coins to the company, and the transaction will be recorded on the blockchain in a matter of seconds. You should then get a confirmation email from the company you purchased from with information about the purchase and the shipping information. As long as you used a legitimate company, you should receive your products just like you would when using PayPal, credit card, or other payment methods.

And that is all that you need to do. Making purchases with Bitcoin is not meant to be difficult, which is why so many people enjoy using this method compared to some of the other options. They get the benefits of using a quick payment method without having to provide all their personal information or worrying like they do when making purchases with credit cards.

Companies that accept Bitcoin

The number of companies who currently accept Bitcoin may not be large, but as more and more people start to use this digital currency, it is likely to grow. There are already a number of companies who already accept Bitcoin and can make it really easy for you to purchase the things you want or need without having to use your traditional currency. Some of the major companies who currently accept Bitcoin include:

- **Bitcoin Coffee:** This is an Alabama company that offers customers a variety of teas and coffees. The default on the website of this company is to show prices in Bitcoin because it values the privacy of its customers, but you can also use a credit card as well.

- **Foodler**: Foodler is a company that offers you online ordering for delivery from many restaurants. It recently announced this year that it would accept Bitcoin as a form of payment for these deliveries. If you are feeling hungry for something in your area, you can order on Foodler and use your Bitcoin now.

- **Pacific Tradewinds Hostel**: If you are traveling in the San Francisco area, you will no longer have to worry about the exchange rate of your national currency. The Tradewinds Hostel in that area will now accept Bitcoin to help make the payments to stay there and to keep the fees low.

- **A-Class Limousine:** this is the only limousine company in New York that will accept Bitcoins. You can choose to work with other methods as well, but this company advertises how using Bitcoin can save the user time and even money on fees compared to other methods.

- **Mega:** Mega is known as a cloud-based data storage provider that can help you to store your private information safe from others. It has set up what is known as a Bitvoucher which has made it possible to pay for your upgrades with Bitcoins, but you can also use PayPal and credit cards as well. Paying with Bitcoin can be nice with this option is nice because you can avoid having to share your personal information while making a payment.

- **OkCupid:** In April, OKCupid started to accept Bitcoin as one of its payment methods. This made it one of the biggest brands to accept the digital currency. According to the CEO of OkCupid, digital currencies are part of the future, and their company wants to be out in the front as well.

- **WordPress:** WordPress was one of the earliest to accept digital currencies. It has always been a company that wanted to be readily available to people all around the world, and most payment methods make this difficult. Just by accepting PayPal, they blocked access from more than 60 countries throughout the world. With Bitcoin, anyone would be able to use WordPress no matter where they are located.

These are just a few of the companies that currently accept Bitcoin, and as time goes on, it is likely that many other companies will start to accept Bitcoin as well. You simply need to click on the link that they provide and send the money over to the company for your payment, or, if you can go in person, you can use your smartphone to send the money over just like with other payment methods. As these digital currencies continue to grow, it is likely that you will see Bitcoin in a variety of places, even at your local grocery store.

Chapter 7: The Way Bitcoin Transactions Work

The main reason that people decide to work with Bitcoin is that it can be used as a payment method. They may be tired of working with credit cards and other online payment methods that are not that secure and easy for them to use. They may choose Bitcoin to keep their transactions secure and safe along with all the other great benefits that come along with it.

Most people come into the Bitcoin network, sign up, exchange out the currency that they want to use, and then they make purchases at the stores that are accepting Bitcoin. They don't think much about how the transactions with Bitcoin really work. They know that they can make a purchase and the transaction is going to be done pretty quickly, but they are not able to explain how these transactions get done so quickly or why they stay secure for everyone on the network.

The blockchain technology that we talked about before is the main reason that transactions work on the Bitcoin network. The blockchain works as a type of ledger on this network. It can technically hold onto information about anything of value, but for Bitcoin, this is usually going to be a transfer of coins between the different users. The blockchain has the benefit of being transparent and secure.

In terms of being transparent, the blockchain is available for anyone on the network to look through. If you have signed up for a Bitcoin address and have some coins, you can look on the blockchain and see these transactions. This helps to keep transparency because you will always be able to see what has been going on with the market, and it is hard for someone to mess with this ledger no matter how hard they try.

The blockchain is also secure. Just because your information is on the ledger doesn't mean people will automatically be able to see what transactions you are completing all the time. The miners come into the game here and will provide unique codes for the blockchain. These codes are important because they hide the information about your transactions while making it impossible for someone to come onto the network and change up the information on the ledger.

Let's look at how this all works. When you sign up for the Bitcoin network, you will automatically receive a chain of your own. This is going to hold onto your transactions on the network including all your purchase, transfers, and the money that you receive from others. Each chain can hold onto a certain number of transactions. The more active you are on the network, the faster you will fill up the chain while those who don't do a lot of transactions could hold onto the same chain for a long time. Once you have filled up one chain, the network will send another one over to you, and the process continues the whole time you are on the Bitcoin network.

Now it is time for the miners to get to work. When your chain gets filled up, it contains all the information about the transactions that you have done. It will include the coins you used, your Bitcoin address, and the Bitcoin address of the person who did the transaction with you. Most people do not want all this personal information to stay on the chain, or it makes things easier for a hacker to gain access to their wallets.

The miners are going to come in here and make sure to change up the information in the chain so that it becomes a unique code and your information will stay secure and safe. There are a number of rules that they have to follow to make these codes. For example, each character of the code needs to be dependent on each other so if one character changes, it will change up all the other parts of the code as well. It also needs to match up with the code already present in the permanent blockchain. This can be challenging, but the point is to make it obvious is someone got on the market and tried to make changes or hide information.

Once a miner is successful with the work they are doing, they will be rewarded with some Bitcoin. They will receive 25 Bitcoin, which can be quite a reward with the current value of this currency and can be a good incentive to help the miners get to work for the market. The users are also going to feel better knowing that the information about their transactions will stay secure even though they are on the blockchain.

After a code has been added to their chain and it is approved by the Bitcoin network, this chain is going to be added to the permanent record of the blockchain. You will be able to check on your transactions any time that you would like, and others can check as well if they need. But your personal information will stay secure and be almost impossible for others to see because of the work of the miner.

This method is really secure and will prevent people from messing around and trying to fake transactions, something that has been difficult to prevent in most big financial institutions. If someone tries to change up one of the chains that are already completed, it is going to mess up the whole code, and anyone will be able to see that something is wrong. For any changes to be approved, over half the computers on the network need to agree to this. Since half the users around the world are not likely to agree at once, and a hacker can't take over these many computers at once, you know the transactions on the blockchain are pretty secure.

The blockchain technology really helps to keep things safe on the Bitcoin network. It is the ledger that will hold onto all the information about all your transactions while also keeping the information private so no one can track you or take your coins from you. While there are many other things that this blockchain technology can be used for, it is really innovative as a way to add trust into the Bitcoin network, as well as into the networks for other digital currencies.

Chapter 8: Bitcoin Use by Businesses

So far in this guidebook, we have been discussing how individuals will choose to use Bitcoin. Many individuals like to use Bitcoin because it makes it easy to perform purchases and send money without having to give up your personal information and the transactions can be completed really quickly. Bitcoin can be a great investment opportunity as well because the value is quickly going up. But if you are a business, whether big or small, you may be wondering whether you should choose to add Bitcoin as one of your accepted payment methods.

There are already several big companies who use Bitcoin as their payment method. They have found that this helps to put them in front of the competition and widens their demographic faster than any other method. And accepting Bitcoin can be easy and painless to do.

Working with Bitcoin can be pretty easy. You simply need to sign up for your own Bitcoin address and set up a wallet so that your customers have a place to send the coins. Then you can add a button to your website so that customers can click and choose to pay with Bitcoin. After the button has been pushed, it is up to you to send out the Bitcoin address you have to them, and they can complete the transaction by instantly sending the coins over to your wallet. You will be able to check on the transaction and see that it has been transferred over in just a few minutes. It is safe, secure, and can help to prevent issues with fraud on both sides.

With Bitcoin still being relatively new, it has only been in the past few years that Bitcoin has really started to grow and since it is one of the first of its kind, many are not sure how it is going to do in the future. This can make some businesses worry about whether Bitcoin is the right option for them or if they should decide to not work with it at all. Let's take a look at some of the risks and some of the benefits of working with Bitcoin so you can decide if accepting Bitcoin as payment is the right choice for you.

The benefits of working with Bitcoin

If you are a business who is considering accepting Bitcoin as a form of payment, there are a lot of benefits that you will be able to enjoy. Bitcoin makes it easy for businesses to accept this digital currency as a form of payment, which makes things easier for the business as well as their customers.

The first benefit that you will find is that you get to choose your own fees. The business will not have to deal with any fees to receive Bitcoins, so you only need to worry about the low fees that come with some wallets. Most wallets will have a low default fee, and you can change this based on how fast you would like to have confirmation of the transactions. The good news is that these fees are going to be unrelated to how much is transferred so it will not vary based on how much the customer spends.

As a business, you probably have had to deal with fraud issues when you accept PayPal and credit cards. Customers can send in a payment and then reverse them on you, costing you a lot of money. With Bitcoin, you are working with a payment method that is secure and irreversible. This means that the cost of fraud is not going to affect your business as much any longer and you will not have to transfer that into higher costs to your customers.

Many businesses reach customers all around the world. Bitcoin can make sending coins between borders easy. You will not have to wait three or more days to complete the transactions, and even if the customer is in another country, you will not have to deal with extra fees for these transfers. You don't even need to worry about having a maximum or minimum amount that has to be sent with these transactions so payments across borders can be simple.

Since Bitcoin is growing so much, there are tons of new customers who are looking for companies that will accept their Bitcoins. When you decide to accept Bitcoins as a form of payment in your shop, you are increasing your visibility and making it easier to reach new customers. This is one of the most cost-effective methods to reach your customers without having to spend thousands on advertising and social media.

The risks of working with Bitcoin

While there are some great benefits to working with Bitcoin, it is not the best for everyone. There are some businesses who are worried about the volatility that comes with this kind of network. They see all the excitement, but then they also see how the value of Bitcoin has seen recent movements down as well and that makes them nervous.

The issue with these big ups and downs for business is that they may have trouble pricing their items for customers. If they put one price on an item and accept payment for it, and then the value of Bitcoin goes down the next day by quite a bit, the business would lose a lot of money in the process, especially if they were not able to withdraw the money before the market went down. That is a huge risk for a business to take. Most business owners do not have the time to watch the market all the time to make sure that the volatility will not make them lose too much money in the process.

As Bitcoin continues to grow, many new businesses are deciding that accepting this digital currency is a good idea. It opens up their target audience so that they can reach more customers in the process. It is an easy payment method that anyone can use and can save them issues with security and privacy. While it may not be the best method for all businesses and it has taken some time to catch on with businesses, it is likely to gain in popularity, and it will not be long before customers can find more companies that are accepting this digital currency.

Chapter 9: Bitcoin and Hacking

It is important that you find some safe and secure ways to protect your Bitcoin if you decide to join the market. Many hackers are seeing the value of these digital coins, and if you do not protect your coins, they will get onto your wallet and steal all the coins. Without any regulatory agencies around, you are out of luck if someone ends up taking your coins.

The good news is there are a few methods that you can use that will help keep your coins safe. Many beginners are going to set up an online wallet, such as using the wallet available on Coinbase because it is easy to work with and can be convenient to leave the coins online. But this is not the safest place to keep your coins. The online wallets have been pretty safe so far, but since they are available online, hackers are constantly trying to get onto the network and get the information that they want.

Moving the coins offline, especially if you plan to use the buy and hold strategy and will not use the coins for some time, can help to keep them safer. Using a hardware wallet, a cold storage wallet, and learning how to stay anonymous will help to ensure that you keep total control over all your coins, no matter how hard the hackers try.

Using a hardware wallet

It may be more convenient to keep your coins online, but if there is a computer glitch or a hacker gets into your wallet, you could lose all your money in no time. This is why many people choose to use a hardware wallet. The hardware wallet is nice because it takes the private key offline, but it is still present on your computer for easy access when you need. You simply need to download a hardware wallet and store the private key inside that file. Some people also choose to download the file onto a USB drive to take it off the computer as well.

Of course, it is a good idea for you to add a password to the file that holds this wallet. And make sure that your computer is up to date with the best antivirus software. If a hacker can gain access to your computer, they could still get ahold of your private key if you are not prepared.

Using cold storage

Cold storage is probably one of the most secure methods to use when it comes to storing your coins away from hackers. For this to work, you will take the private key and print it off your computer. This effectively leaves your key offline and off your computer. Unless the hacker physically comes to your home, they will not be able to access the private key that you have.

With this method, you need to store the paper in a secure location. It will not do you much good to print off the private key and then lose the paper. Storing in a folder that you will not lose or in a safety deposit box will help you to keep the key as safe as possible. Any time that you purchase more coins to add to your wallet, make sure to print off the key again so that it is updated.

Remaining anonymous

It is important to remember that these digital currencies are available online and while the blockchain technology does its best to keep your information safe and secure, you need to take extra precautions as well. The first precaution that you should use is to come up with a unique address. This address is what you will use any time that you want to send and receive coins on the network. If you put some personal information in the address, such as your first and last name, you make it easy for a hacker to track your transactions right back to their origin.

Make sure that you pick out an address that is completely unique. You can create one on your own or use some of the generators that are online to help you out. Also, if you plan on doing lots of transactions through the Bitcoin network, it may be a good idea to change your address on occasion. Hackers will always look for patterns in the market, for things that look familiar and if you use the same address for a lot of transactions, they can still track it back to you. Switch the address on occasion to keep your coins safe.

With the growth of digital currencies, especially with Bitcoin, hackers are always looking to figure out how to get into a users wallet and steal their coins. And once the hacker gains access to the wallet, it is going to be really hard for you to get your coins back. Taking the right precautions and backing up your private key will ensure that you always have access to your coins, no matter what happens on the network.

Chapter 10: Future of Bitcoin

While Bitcoin has become a household name over the past year or so, it really has not been around that long. Started in 2009, there has been a lot of growth, and many other digital currencies have sprouted out because of this particular currency. But this leaves a lot of people around the world wondering; what is going to happen with Bitcoin in the future?

Some people are worried that Bitcoin is not going to be able to handle the amount of interest that will come to it in the future. Already there have been some signs of issues with Bitcoin because there are so many people who are interested in working with this currency. The blockchain technology as it is currently set up, and the limited number of coins that are available, could pose some problems with the system. Already there are some issues with how long processing time occurs depending on how many people are on the network, and this could spell more issues for this large currency.

There have already been a few splits within the Bitcoin network. Some want to keep Bitcoin exactly how it was designed, refusing to change up the technology that is behind Bitcoin or add on any more coins to the network. Others think that some changes need to be made to keep Bitcoin prevalent on the market so that people will not run away from it. These clashing thoughts led to a split between the company, and now there is Bitcoin and Bitcoin Cash. They work in similar manners and if you have Bitcoin and want to switch over to Bitcoin Cash without many problems.

As Bitcoin continues to grow and people see that there is some volatility in this market, there are some who are choosing to go with other currencies. Not all digital currencies work the same way that Bitcoin. Bitcoin is a payment method, but there are other options, and these can quickly attract different users based on why they want to use the currency. And if Bitcoin keeps having some troubles inside the company and with the blockchain, it is likely that another digital currency could take over in the future.

One of the biggest problems that Bitcoin, as well as the other digital currencies, are facing is regulations from governments. While Bitcoin is decentralized and does not require any help from a central government, this has not stopped governments in various countries from setting up rules and requirement for users of digital currencies in their countries.

Each country is different, but let's look at how the United States government is reacting to these currencies. In the United States, the government has started to step in and require that all exchange sites receiver personal information on any user who is switching out their traditional currency for a cryptocurrency like Bitcoin. This personal information is supposed to help prevent illegal activities like money laundering and tax evasion, but it takes away some of the benefits that come with using digital currencies; namely, that the user wants to go on the network and remain anonymous.

The United State has also required that some of their allies put more stringent rules and regulations on digital currencies in other countries to help prevent the sales of illegal arms and other materials. The United States is just one of the countries to go against Bitcoin and other digital currencies in this manner and the more rules and regulations that are placed on these currencies, the harder it will be for users to join the networks, and this can definitely affect currencies like Bitcoin.

Overall, it is estimated that despite some of these setbacks, currencies like Bitcoin are going to keep growing. There is a large market for these currencies, and there are many different benefits to using these currencies. The large increases that are occurring now are not likely to continue in the future, but it is unlikely that these currencies are going anywhere soon.

Conclusion

Thank you for making it through to the end of this book, land I hope it was informative and able to provide you with all of the tools you need to achieve your goals in reading up on Bitcoin.

The next step is to decide whether you would like to work with Bitcoin or not. There are a lot of benefits, and it is going to the future with an even stronger pull as more and more people hear about how it works. While some join the market simply to invest and make money with this currency while it grows, others are joining because it is a convenient method of payment no matter where they are located throughout the world.

In this book I spent some time looking at Bitcoin and all of the neat things that you can do with it. Whether you want to use Bitcoin to make purchases, you are a business considering accepting Bitcoin, or you want to make money off Bitcoin, you will learn all the answers to your questions inside this guidebook.

Bitcoin is likely to grow more and more into the future. Learning how it works and understanding some of the benefits of going with this currency rather than one of the other options can make a big difference in the results that you get. When you are ready to join the Bitcoin network, read through this guidebook and learn exactly how to get started today!

Finally, if you found this book useful, I would be grateful if you leave a review on Amazon.

Thank you for purchasing my book.

www.ingramcontent.com/pod-product-compliance
Lightning Source LLC
Chambersburg PA
CBHW072048230526
45468CB00019B/1043